About the Author

Mr. Paul Watson is a technology enthusiast and has massive experience in various technologies like web application development, automation testing, build automation, continuous integration and deployment technologies. He has worked on most of the technology stacks.

He has hands on experience on UFT, LeanFT, Selenium and Appium. He has used testing frameworks like JUnit, TestNG, Cucumber with Selenium. He has also worked on Struts, Spring, Bootstratp, Angular JS.

Who is this book for

This book is for software developers, automation testers, Devops and engineers working on IT project. Whether you are a beginner or an experienced developer, this book will help you master the skills on Git.

The book starts with introduction of Git and then dives into key concepts like Branching and merging, resolving conflicts, pushing and pulling to remote repositories and integration with IntelliJ IDEA.

What is covered in this book

1. This book covers below topics on Bamboo.
2. Installing Git
3. Understanding Git architecture
4. Creating new Git repository
5. Viewing Git configuration, First time Git configuration
6. Using SSH keys with Git
7. Checking Git status
8. Adding files into staging area in Git
9. Committing changes to the local repository
10. Ignoring files using .gitignore
11. Viewing the history of commits
12. Viewing the file contents in working directory, staging area and repository
13. Viewing difference between files
14. Viewing the history of files
15. Git revert and Git Reset
16. Getting back deleted commits using git reflog
17. Managing branches
18. Collaborating with team
19. Stashing the changes in Git
20. Tags in Git
21. Patches in Git
22. Working with GitHub project
23. Git integration

Table of Contents

1. Introduction

GIT is the most popular version control system.

Key features of GIT are -

1. Distributed
2. Open source
3. Cross platform
4. Supports branching and merging
5. Multiple workflows like linear, central
6. Staging area

2. Installation

Now let us see how to install the git.

Visit git official download page and download the git for your platform.

On windows, you will download exe file. Just double click on it and installation process will start.

Once the installation is complete, add the git directory to the path environment variable as shown in below image.

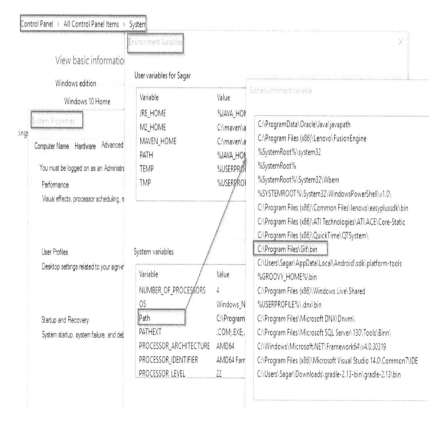

Updating path variable to point to git bin directory

To check that git is installed properly, open the git bash and type below command.

git --version

If everything is good, you should see output similar to below image.

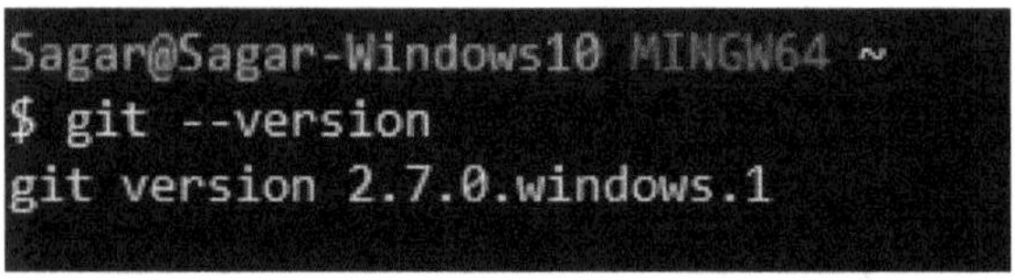

git version command

Congrats! you have just installed git successfully.

3. Understanding Git architecture

Git is a distributed VCS. When a developer creates new repository or clones existing one, he gets his own copy of the entire repository on his machine. He can make commits to local repository and once all changes are finished, he can push that to remote repository.

Below image shows how the entire architecture of Git looks like.

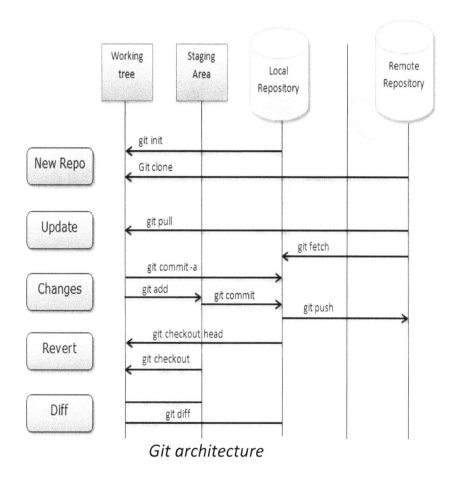

Git architecture

4. Creating new Git repository

4.1 Initializing new Git repository

To create new git repository, you can use below command.

git init

Below image shows sample output of above command. Notice that you should run this command from within the project directory.

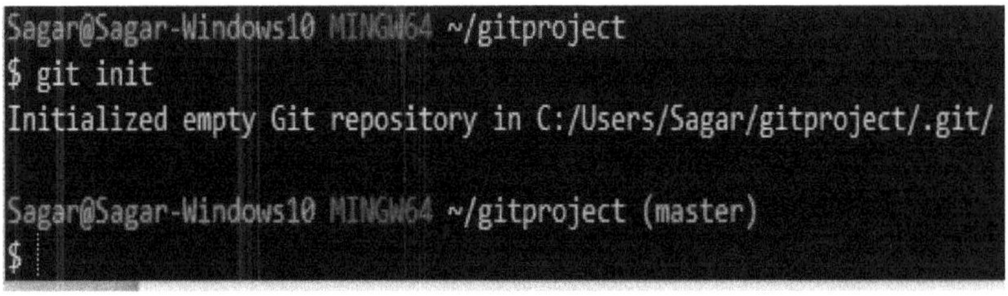

Initializing new Git repository

After running this command, you will notice that .git directory is created inside gitproject directory.

· gitproject > .git

Name

   hooks
   info
   objects
   refs
   config
   description
   HEAD

.git directory after executing git init command

4.2 Cloning new Git repository

In this article, let us see how to clone git repository.

Below commands will clone the remote git repository on your local machine.

1. git clone git@github.com:reply2sagar/gitproject.git : It uses the SSH protocol. Ensure that you have set up SSH keys properly before using this protocol.

2. https://github.com/reply2sagar/gitproject.git : It uses the https protocol. You will have to enter user Id and password for authentication.

```
Sagar@Sagar-Windows10 MINGW64 ~
$ git clone git@github.com:reply2sagar/gitproject.git
Cloning into 'gitproject'...
remote: Counting objects: 23, done.
remote: Compressing objects: 100% (12/12), done.
remote: Total 23 (delta 2), reused 20 (delta 2), pack-reused 0
Receiving objects: 100% (23/23), done.
Resolving deltas: 100% (2/2), done.
Checking connectivity... done.
```

git clone

```
Sagar@Sagar-Windows10 MINGW64 ~
$ cd gitproject

Sagar@Sagar-Windows10 MINGW64 ~/gitproject (master)
$ ls
abc  f1.txt  x.txt

Sagar@Sagar-Windows10 MINGW64 ~/gitproject (master)
$ ls -a
./  ../  .git/  .gitignore  abc  f1.txt  x.txt
```

viewing cloned git repository

4.3 .git directory in Git repository

.git directory stores all important information about the Git repository.

11

It is present in your git repository directory as shown in below image.

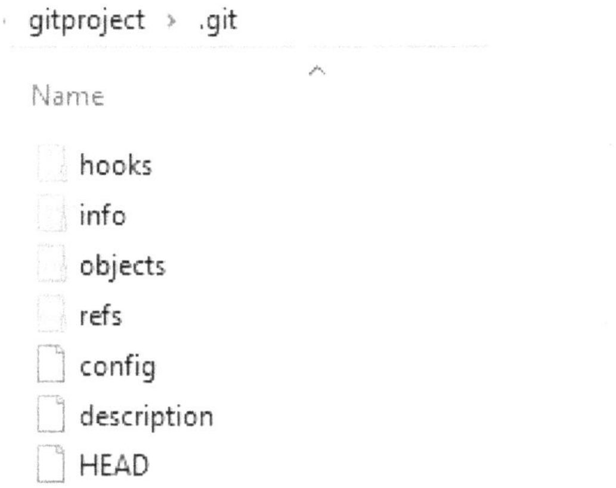

gitproject > .git

Name

hooks
info
objects
refs
config
description
HEAD

.git directory

Let us take a look at the significance of each of these files and directories.

1. hooks - actions to be takes after certain event like commit, update etc.
2. info
3. objects
4. refs - list of all refs like heads, tags etc
5. config - tells if repository is bare or not. Also contains lot of configuration settings like user name, email address, remotes
6. description - Name of the repository
7. HEAD - current ref

5. Git configuration

5.1 Viewing Git configuration

Git configuration is stored at 3 levels.

1. System - These settings apply to all Git repositories created by all users of the system. On windows, you might find system config file at C:\ProgramData\Git. On Linux machine, System config file is located at /etc/gitconfig.
2. User (Global) - These settings apply to all Git repositories created by specific user. This file is located at user home directory. Sometimes it is available at user home directory (on network).
3. Local - These settings apply to single repository.

Below commands are used to view various Git settings.

1. git config --system --list
2. git config --global --list
3. git config --local --list
4. git config –l

Below commands are used to edit various Git settings.

1. git config --system --edit
2. git config --global --edit
3. git config --local --edit

If you do not like typing the commands, you can directly open these files in text editor to view and edit them.

Below images show sample output of above commands.

```
Sagar@Sagar-Windows10 MINGW64 ~/gitproject (master)
$ git config --list
core.symlinks=false
core.autocrlf=true
color.diff=auto
color.status=auto
color.branch=auto
color.interactive=true
help.format=html
http.sslcainfo=C:/Program Files/Git/mingw64/ssl/certs/ca-bundle.crt
diff.astextplain.textconv=astextplain
rebase.autosquash=true
user.name=sagar
user.email=sagar@softpost.com
user.autocrlf=false
pusg.default=simple
push.default=simple
core.autocrlf=true
core.repositoryformatversion=0
core.filemode=false
core.bare=false
core.logallrefupdates=true
core.symlinks=false
core.ignorecase=true
core.hidedotfiles=dotGitOnly
```

Viewing git configuration

```
Sagar@Sagar-Windows10 MINGW64 ~/gitproject (master)
$ git config --list --global
user.name=sagar
user.email=sagar@softpost.com
user.autocrlf=false
pusg.default=simple
push.default=simple
core.autocrlf=true
```

Viewing global git configuration settings

```
Sagar@Sagar-Windows10 MINGW64 ~/gitproject (master)
$ git config --list --local
core.repositoryformatversion=0
core.filemode=false
core.bare=false
core.logallrefupdates=true
core.symlinks=false
core.ignorecase=true
core.hidedotfiles=dotGitOnly
```

Viewing local git configuration settings

15

5.2 First time git configuration settings

You can configure your user name and email address using below commands.

git config --global user.name "sagar"

git config --global user.email "sagar@softpost.com"

To view if the settings are applied properly, you can use below commands.

git config --list

git config user.name

git config user.email

6. Using SSH keys with Git

We can communicate with Git repository using 2 main protocols.

1. HTTP
2. SSH

The disadvantage of using HTTP protocol is that every time you access the remote repository, you will have to enter user id and password for authentication purpose. To avoid typing the password, you can use SSH protocol.

You need to follow below steps to set up SSH keys for authentication purpose.

1. Create pair of public and private keys using ssh-keygen command
2. Add private key to the SSH agent running on local machine
3. Add public key on the Git server like Stash or GitHub.

Generating SSH keys

Below command is used to create SSH keys.

ssh-keygen -t rsa -b 4096 -C "sagar@softpost.org"

Above command creates pair of keys - public (id_rsa.pub) and private (id_rsa) in .ssh directory under your home directory.

Registering private key with SSH agent on local machine

Below command will start the SSH agent.

eval "$(ssh-agent -s)"

Below command will register the private ssh key with agent.

ssh-add ~/.ssh/id_rsa

Adding the public key on Git server

You have to copy the public key from the id_rsa.pub file and paste it on the server SSH key section. Below image shows sample key added on GitHub.

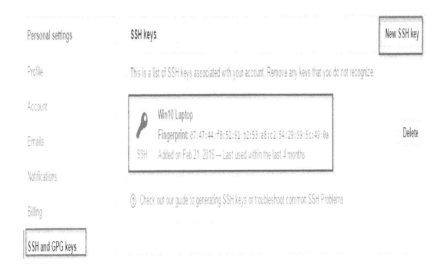

SSH keys on GitHub

7. Checking Git status

One of the most frequently used Git command is - git status.

This command gives lot of useful information as mentioned below.

1. tells which branch you are on. By default you are on master branch.
2. tracked files/ untracked files if any
3. If there are any files in the staging area ready to be committed.
4. also tells if there is any conflict when you are merging 2 branches.
5. tells if local branch is ahead or behind of remote tracking branch.

Below image shows sample output of git status command. Notice that after creating new file, git status command shows that file in untracked files section.

```
Sagar@Sagar-Windows10 MINGW64 ~/gitproject (master)
$ git status
On branch master

Initial commit

nothing to commit (create/copy files and use "git add" to track)

Sagar@Sagar-Windows10 MINGW64 ~/gitproject (master)
$ vi f1.txt

Sagar@Sagar-Windows10 MINGW64 ~/gitproject (master)
$ git status
On branch master

Initial commit

Untracked files:
  (use "git add <file>..." to include in what will be committed)

        f1.txt

nothing added to commit but untracked files present (use "git add" to track)

Sagar@Sagar-Windows10 MINGW64 ~/gitproject (master)
$
```

git status command output

8. Adding files into staging area in Git

As mentioned in the article on Git architecture, we know that Git has one feature called as Staging area.

Staging area contains the list of changes that will be committed into the repository. So before committing anything into repository, you have to add the files into staging area.

Below image would be useful to understand the staging area (Also called as index or cache)

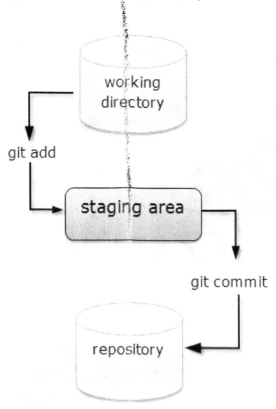

Staging area in Git

Below command shows sample output of git add command. Note that we had one untracked file - f1.txt

To add this file into staging area, we have used **git add f1.txt** command. After the file is added into staging area, git status shows that file in changes to be committed section.

```
Sagar@Sagar-Windows10 MINGW64 ~/gitproject (master)
$ git status
On branch master

Initial commit

Untracked files:
  (use "git add <file>..." to include in what will be committed)

        f1.txt

nothing added to commit but untracked files present (use "git add" to track)

Sagar@Sagar-Windows10 MINGW64 ~/gitproject (master)
$ git add f1.txt
warning: LF will be replaced by CRLF in f1.txt.
The file will have its original line endings in your working directory.

Sagar@Sagar-Windows10 MINGW64 ~/gitproject (master)
$ git status
On branch master

Initial commit

Changes to be committed:
  (use "git rm --cached <file>..." to unstage)

        new file:   f1.txt
```

git add command

More add commands -

1. git add . : adds everything to staging area except removed files
2. git add -u: adds everything except new files
3. git add -A : It is as good as above 2 commands combined together

9. Committing changes to the local repository

Changes that are in the staging area are committed to repository. To commit the changes, you have to use **git commit** command.

Below image shows the commit command in action. Notice that we had one file in staging area - f1.txt

After commit command is executed, nothing remains in staging area. So git status says that nothing to commit. Also In working directory, there are no new changes. If we modify, delete or add new files in the working directory, git status will give proper information.

```
$ git status
On branch master

Initial commit

Changes to be committed:
  (use "git rm --cached <file>..." to unstage)

        new file:   f1.txt


Sagar@Sagar-Windows10 MINGW64 ~/gitproject (master)
$ git commit -m "First commit"
[master (root-commit) 5d98801] First commit
warning: LF will be replaced by CRLF in f1.txt.
The file will have its original line endings in your working directory.
 1 file changed, 1 insertion(+)
 create mode 100644 f1.txt

Sagar@Sagar-Windows10 MINGW64 ~/gitproject (master)
$ git status
On branch master
nothing to commit, working directory clean
```

committing the changes to local repository

10. Ignoring files using .gitignore

By default, all files that we add to working directory are tracked by Git. But sometimes, we do not bother about changes in those files. For example - Consider maven project. When the project is built using maven, it creates target directory. We are not interested in storing this directory and all it's contents.

How to tell Git not to track specific files? That's when .gitignore comes into picture.

.gitignore is the special file that can be created and stored in the root of the Git repository. It contains the list of files or directories that should be ignored.

Here is the sample .gitignore file contents for various types of Java project. Notice that to ignore directory and its entire contents you have to use / at the end of directory name.

```
# Files to be ignored for IntelliJ IDEA Project
.idea/
*.iml
*.iws
```

```
# Files to be ignored for Maven Project
target/
log/
```

```
# Files to be ignored for Eclipse Project
.classpath
.project
```

#To ignore all files ending with .xml

*.xml

Below example shows that even though we create and change the XML file, Git does not track it as we have added *.xml line in .gitignore file.

```
Sagar@Sagar-Windows10 MINGW64 ~/gitproject (master)
$ vi abc.xml

Sagar@Sagar-Windows10 MINGW64 ~/gitproject (master)
$ git status
On branch master
nothing to commit, working directory clean

Sagar@Sagar-Windows10 MINGW64 ~/gitproject (master)
$ cat .gitignore
*.xml

Sagar@Sagar-Windows10 MINGW64 ~/gitproject (master)
$
```

gitignore example in Git

11. Viewing the history of commits

Git repository can be considered as a chain of commits as shown in below image. In below image, C1 is the first commit. C2 is the second commit. C2 will point to C1. If we add on more commit say C3, C3 will point to C2.

There is special pointer called as HEAD which always points to the currently checked out commit.

Git repository as a chain of commits

If you want to view the history of Git commits, you can use below command.

git log

Below image shows that current branch of the repository has 2 commits. For each commit, it shows below information.

1. Commit hash id
2. Author of the commit
3. Time stamp when the commit was made
4. Commit message

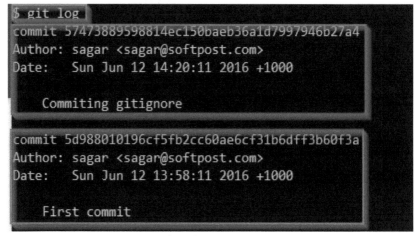

```
$ git log
commit 57473889598814ec150baeb36a1d7997946b27a4
Author: sagar <sagar@softpost.com>
Date:   Sun Jun 12 14:20:11 2016 +1000

    Commiting gitignore

commit 5d988010196cf5fb2cc60ae6cf31b6dff3b60f3a
Author: sagar <sagar@softpost.com>
Date:   Sun Jun 12 13:58:11 2016 +1000

    First commit
```

git log history

git log command accepts lot of parameters as mentioned below.

1. git log -3 : This shows only last 3 commits
2. git log --author="sagar" : This shows only commits made by specific author say sagar
3. git log --after="2016-06-12 14:37" --before="2016-06-12 15:59" : This shows commits made only between 12 June 2016 14:37 to 12 June 2016 15:59
4. git log --all --grep "[abc|xyz]" : shows all commits where commit message matches the given regular expression.
5. git log --graph --oneline --decorate --all : shows git history in graphical format
6. git log --pretty=oneline : Shows git history in one line per commit
7. git log --name-status : shows which files have changed in each commit

29

8. git show --pretty="format:" --name-
   only 878sdjhsk8 : shows which files have changed
   in git in specific commit

```
$ git log --after="2016-06-12 14:00" --before="2016-06-12 15:00"
commit 57473889598814ec150baeb36a1d7997946b27a4
Author: sagar <sagar@softpost.com>
Date:   Sun Jun 12 14:20:11 2016 +1000

    Commiting gitignore

Sagar@Sagar-Windows10 MINGW64 ~/gitproject (master)
$ git log -1
commit 57473889598814ec150baeb36a1d7997946b27a4
Author: sagar <sagar@softpost.com>
Date:   Sun Jun 12 14:20:11 2016 +1000

    Commiting gitignore

Sagar@Sagar-Windows10 MINGW64 ~/gitproject (master)
$ git log --author="saga"
commit 57473889598814ec150baeb36a1d7997946b27a4
Author: sagar <sagar@softpost.com>
Date:   Sun Jun 12 14:20:11 2016 +1000

    Commiting gitignore

commit 5d988010196cf5fb2cc60ae6cf31b6dff3b60f3a
Author: sagar <sagar@softpost.com>
Date:   Sun Jun 12 13:58:11 2016 +1000

    First commit
```

```
$ git log --all --grep "[commit|Com]"
commit 57473889598814ec150baeb36a1d7997946b27a4
Author: sagar <sagar@softpost.com>
Date:   Sun Jun 12 14:20:11 2016 +1000

    Commiting gitignore

commit 5d988010196cf5fb2cc60ae6cf31b6dff3b60f3a
Author: sagar <sagar@softpost.com>
Date:   Sun Jun 12 13:58:11 2016 +1000

    First commit
```

Viewing the commits by message in all branches

12. Viewing the file contents

Below image shows how to view contents of same file in working directory, staging area and repository.

Notice how we can see the historical versions of file using HEAD^1 syntax.

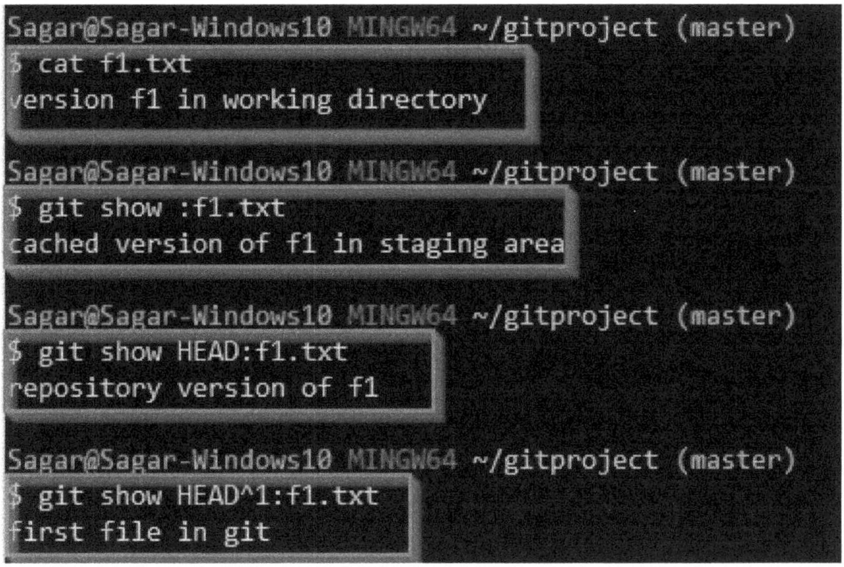

```
Sagar@Sagar-Windows10 MINGW64 ~/gitproject (master)
$ cat f1.txt
version f1 in working directory

Sagar@Sagar-Windows10 MINGW64 ~/gitproject (master)
$ git show :f1.txt
cached version of f1 in staging area

Sagar@Sagar-Windows10 MINGW64 ~/gitproject (master)
$ git show HEAD:f1.txt
repository version of f1

Sagar@Sagar-Windows10 MINGW64 ~/gitproject (master)
$ git show HEAD^1:f1.txt
first file in git
```

Viewing various versions of file

13. Viewing difference between files

git diff command can be used to view the difference between files in Git.

1. git diff : shows the difference between working directory and staging area
2. git diff --cached : shows the difference between staging area and HEAD (last commit)
3. git diff HEAD : shows the difference between working directory and HEAD (last commit)
4. git diff HEAD^1 : shows the difference between working directory and HEAD (second last commit)
5. git diff --name-only :shows only the list of files that have changed in working directory since last commit
6. gitk f1.txt : shows the difference in GUI

Below image shows how to view difference between files in Working directory, staging area and HEAD (last commit in repository).

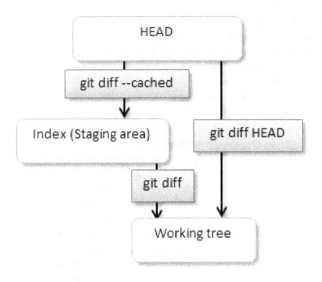

Viewing difference between files in Git

Below image shows the sample output of above commands. Lines in red color means that line is not available in source file. Lines in green color means that line is available in source file but not in destination file.

```
$ git diff
diff --git a/f1.txt b/f1.txt
index efbcf2a..16c1f12 100644
--- a/f1.txt
+++ b/f1.txt
@@ -1 +1 @@
-cached version of f1 in staging area
+version f1 in working directory
warning: LF will be replaced by CRLF in f1.txt.
The file will have its original line endings in your working directory.

Sagar@Sagar-Windows10 MINGW64 ~/gitproject (master)
$ git diff HEAD
diff --git a/f1.txt b/f1.txt
index 4c87769..16c1f12 100644
--- a/f1.txt
+++ b/f1.txt
@@ -1 +1 @@
-repository version of f1
+version f1 in working directory
warning: LF will be replaced by CRLF in f1.txt.
The file will have its original line endings in your working directory.

Sagar@Sagar-Windows10 MINGW64 ~/gitproject (master)
$ git diff --cached
diff --git a/f1.txt b/f1.txt
index 4c87769..efbcf2a 100644
--- a/f1.txt
+++ b/f1.txt
@@ -1 +1 @@
-repository version of f1
+cached version of f1 in staging area
```

git diff commands

Below image shows how gitk tool looks like.

gitk f1.txt

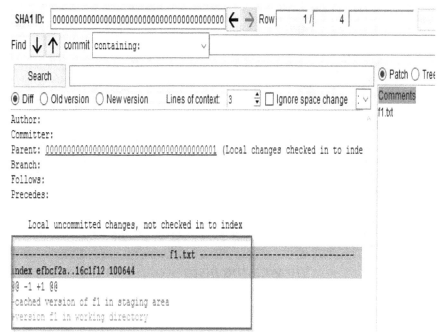

Viewing difference between files using gitk

14. Viewing the history of files

We can use git show command to view the history of file.

1. cat f1.txt = shows the file contents as in working directory
2. git show :f1.txt = shows the contents of the file in staging area
3. git show HEAD:f1.txt = shows the contents of the file as in last commit
4. git show HEAD^1:f1.txt = shows the contents of the file as in second last commit

```
Sagar@Sagar-Windows10 MINGW64 ~/gitproject (master)
$ cat f1.txt
version f1 in working directory

Sagar@Sagar-Windows10 MINGW64 ~/gitproject (master)
$ git show :f1.txt
cached version of f1 in staging area

Sagar@Sagar-Windows10 MINGW64 ~/gitproject (master)
$ git show HEAD:f1.txt
repository version of f1

Sagar@Sagar-Windows10 MINGW64 ~/gitproject (master)
$ git show HEAD^1:f1.txt
first file in git
```

Viewing the history of file in Git

15. Git revert and Git Reset

You can revert the last commit in Git using below command.

git revert <commit-id>

Some examples -

git revert 7893dd38bd467d

git revert HEAD

git revert HEAD^

Below example will help you understand how Git revert works. Notice that even though we revert second last commit - Q, other commits R and S are still in the git log history and additional commit T is also created reverting the changes made in commit Q.

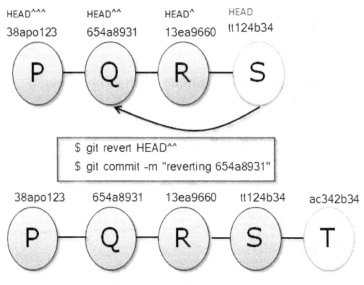

git revert diagram

Below images show how we have reverted the commit starting with Hash id - 7893dd38bd467d. Notice that after reverting the commit, old commit remains in the git log. But **new commit is created and all the changes in the old commit are reverted.**

```
$ git log
commit 7893dd38bd467d8397205da661a6f7a59ef77032
Author: sagar <sagar@softpost.com>
Date:   Sun Jun 19 08:12:54 2016 +1000

    committing f1.txt

commit 5631fb6061d01ddeec8e4226a39dabb3f2fdd122
Author: sagar <sagar@softpost.com>
Date:   Sun Jun 12 14:59:05 2016 +1000

    repo version

commit 57473889598814ec150baeb36a1d7997946b27a4
Author: sagar <sagar@softpost.com>
Date:   Sun Jun 12 14:20:11 2016 +1000

    Commiting gitignore

commit 5d988010196cf5fb2cc60ae6cf31b6dff3b60f3a
Author: sagar <sagar@softpost.com>
Date:   Sun Jun 12 13:58:11 2016 +1000

    First commit
```

git log

```
$ git revert HEAD
[b1 321fe0c] Revert "committing f1.txt"
1 file changed, 1 insertion(+), 1 deletion(-)

Sagar@Sagar-Windows10 MINGW64 ~/gitproject (b1)
$ git log
commit 321fe0c5268ea024fb6a2491a8bbc21749bdd696
Author: sagar <sagar@softpost.com>
Date:   Sun Jun 19 08:13:43 2016 +1000


    Revert "committing f1.txt"


    This reverts commit 7893dd38bd467d8397205da661a6f7a59ef77032.

commit 7893dd38bd467d8397205da661a6f7a59ef77032
Author: sagar <sagar@softpost.com>
Date:   Sun Jun 19 08:12:54 2016 +1000

    committing f1.txt

commit 5631fb6061d01ddeec8e4226a39dabb3f2fdd122
Author: sagar <sagar@softpost.com>
Date:   Sun Jun 12 14:59:05 2016 +1000

    repo version

commit 57473889598814ec150baeb36a1d7997946b27a4
Author: sagar <sagar@softpost.com>
Date:   Sun Jun 12 14:20:11 2016 +1000

    Commiting gitignore

commit 5d988010196cf5fb2cc60ae6cf31b6dff3b60f3a
Author: sagar <sagar@softpost.com>
```

git revert

41

Difference between Git reset and Git revert

In this article, we are going to see the difference between Git reset and Git revert.

As we know that Git revert does not delete the commit from the Git history but creates new commit wherein all changes are reverted from specific commit.

Main difference in Git reset and revert is that in Git reset commit history of Git changes as shown in below image.

Commits with id C3 and C4 are removed if we execute below command.

git reset HEAD^^

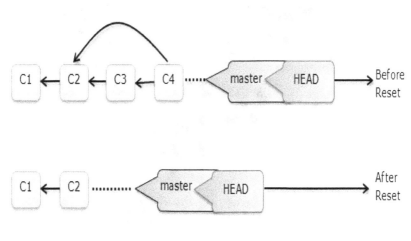

git reset diagram

Below image shows the sample Git log before executing reset command.

```
$ git log
commit 321fe0c5268ea024fb6a2491a8bbc21749bdd696
Author: sagar <sagar@softpost.com>
Date:   Sun Jun 19 08:13:43 2016 +1000

    Revert "committing f1.txt"

    This reverts commit 7893dd38bd467d8397205da661a6f7a5

commit 7893dd38bd467d8397205da661a6f7a59ef77032
Author: sagar <sagar@softpost.com>
Date:   Sun Jun 19 08:12:54 2016 +1000

    committing f1.txt

commit 5631fb6061d01ddeec8e4226a39dabb3f2fdd122
Author: sagar <sagar@softpost.com>
Date:   Sun Jun 12 14:59:05 2016 +1000

    repo version

commit 57473889598814ec150baeb36a1d7997946b27a4
Author: sagar <sagar@softpost.com>
Date:   Sun Jun 12 14:20:11 2016 +1000

    Commiting gitignore

commit 5d988010196cf5fb2cc60ae6cf31b6dff3b60f3a
Author: sagar <sagar@softpost.com>
Date:   Sun Jun 12 13:58:11 2016 +1000

    First commit
```

git log before git reset

Below image shows the sample git log after the git reset command is executed. Notice that last 2 commits have been deleted from git log history.

```
Sagar@Sagar-Windows10 MINGW64 ~/gitproject (b1)
$ git reset HEAD^^

Sagar@Sagar-Windows10 MINGW64 ~/gitproject (b1)
$ git log
commit 5631fb6061d01ddeec8e4226a39dabb3f2fdd122
Author: sagar <sagar@softpost.com>
Date:    Sun Jun 12 14:59:05 2016 +1000

    repo version

commit 57473889598814ec150baeb36a1d7997946b27a4
Author: sagar <sagar@softpost.com>
Date:    Sun Jun 12 14:20:11 2016 +1000

    Commiting gitignore

commit 5d988010196cf5fb2cc60ae6cf31b6dff3b60f3a
Author: sagar <sagar@softpost.com>
Date:    'Sun Jun 12 13:58:11 2016 +1000

    First commit
```

git log after git reset

Hard and Soft reset in Git

1. git reset --hard HEAD~1 – After reset, It removes changes from staging area and working copy.
2. git reset HEAD~1 – After reset, working tree will not be affected. But changes in staging area will be removed.
3. git reset --soft HEAD~1 – After reset, working tree and index (staging area) is not affected.

Some more interesting scenarios -

1. git reset --hard origin/master : resets the local branch to remote master branch

16. Getting back deleted commits using git reflog

When we use git reset, some commits in the git history might be deleted. Suppose you want the changes from some of those deleted commits. Is there any solution?

Yes - that's when **git reflog** command comes into picture.

Below image shows that we have a commit starting with Id **db1a0** in our git History.

deleting last commit using git reset

Below image shows that we have deleted the commit
starting with id **db1a0**

```
Sagar@Sagar-Windows10 MINGW64 ~/gitproject (master)
$ git reset HEAD^
Unstaged changes after reset:
M       abc

Sagar@Sagar-Windows10 MINGW64 ~/gitproject (master)
$ git log -3
commit bfce6b2d91a8ddb1a10899fbed320458b08c1b07
Merge: b21d373 0a307d0
Author: sagar <sagar@softpost.com>
Date:   Sun Jun 19 16:22:33 2016 +1000

    hi

commit b21d373f20bf1d4ee32ff954d83529e4d60e3d0e
Author: sagar <sagar@softpost.com>
Date:   Sun Jun 19 10:07:48 2016 +1000

    committing f1

commit 0a307d03e8caa2b07a1f12b9528f57d8de0b5ea2
Author: sagar <sagar@softpost.com>
Date:   Sun Jun 19 10:07:02 2016 +1000

    committing f1
```

deleting last commit using git reset

Below image shows that we can still view the deleted
commit in git reflog. To get back the changes from that
commit, we can check it out and then merge it into our
branch.

```
$ git reflog
bfce6b2 HEAD@{0}: reset: moving to HEAD^
db1a0b4 HEAD@{1}: pull: Fast-forward
bfce6b2 HEAD@{2}: commit (merge): hi          This commit was deleted from
b21d373 HEAD@{3}: commit: committing f1       git history, but it is available in
5d17222 HEAD@{4}: checkout: moving from x to master   reflog
0a307d0 HEAD@{5}: commit: committing f1
5d17222 HEAD@{6}: checkout: moving from master to x
5d17222 HEAD@{7}: merge x: Fast-forward
5631fb6 HEAD@{8}: checkout: moving from x to master
```

git reflog

17. Managing branches

17.1 Creating and switching to new branches

Branches are used to develop the code independent of main branch.

Main advantages of Git branch are -

2. separates main development work from small tasks.
3. You can easily context switch between different tasks.
4. Allows you to work on specific features or functionalities of the application. You merge your work in main branch only when your branch code is finished and working properly.
5. Allows you to provide hot bug fix easily without affecting what you are doing currently.

To create a branch, you can use below command. It will create a branch with name x. Notice that below command will only create a new branch. That branch will not be checked out in your working copy.

git branch x

To check out above branch in working copy, you have to use below command.

git checkout x

To create a new branch and check it out in working copy at the same time, you have to use below command. It will create new branch b2 and check it out.

git checkout -b b2

```
Sagar@Sagar-Windows10 MINGW64 ~/gitproject (master)
$ git branch x

Sagar@Sagar-Windows10 MINGW64 ~/gitproject (master)
$ git branch
  b1
* master
  x

Sagar@Sagar-Windows10 MINGW64 ~/gitproject (master)
$ git checkout -b b2
Switched to a new branch 'b2'

Sagar@Sagar-Windows10 MINGW64 ~/gitproject (b2)
$ git branch
  b1
* b2
  master
  x

Sagar@Sagar-Windows10 MINGW64 ~/gitproject (b2)
$ git checkout x
Switched to branch 'x'
```

creating new branches and checking out in Git

After a branch is created and checked out, you can make changes to files, add them to staging area or commit them. Once you are finished with all your changes, you can merge your branch in to main branch.

You can also create a branch off specific commit using below syntax.

1. git branch branch-name <commit Id>
2. git branch branch-name HEAD~3
3. git checkout -b new_branch v1.2 : creating branch off tag

17.2 Viewing existing branches

A Git repository can contain multiple branches in it. There are 2 types of branches.

1. Local
2. Remote

Below image shows how to view local and remote branches. It shows that we have 2 branches locally - b1 and master while on remote we have just one branch master.

```
$ git branch
* b1
  master

Sagar@Sagar-Windows10 MINGW64 ~/gitproject (b1)
$ git branch -r
  myorigin/master
```

Viewing existing branches in Git

17.3 Merging branches

We can merge branches in 2 ways.

1. Fast forward
2. 3 way merge

Fast forward merging

Below image shows how the fast forward merge works in Git. From master branch, we created new feature branch and added 2 commits into it. Meanwhile master branch has no new commits. In this case, merging is done by pointing the HEAD to tip of feature branch.

Before Merging

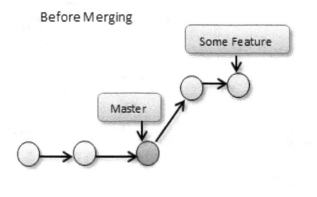

After a Fast-Forward Merge

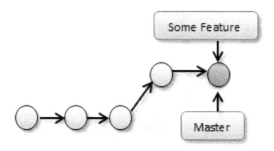

Fast forward merge in Git

```
Sagar@Sagar-Windows10 MINGW64 ~/gitproject (x)
$ git checkout master
Switched to branch 'master'
Your branch is up-to-date with 'myorigin/master'.

Sagar@Sagar-Windows10 MINGW64 ~/gitproject (master)
$ git merge b2
Already up-to-date.

Sagar@Sagar-Windows10 MINGW64 ~/gitproject (master)
$ git merge x
Updating 5631fb6..5d17222
Fast-forward
```

Merging branch using fast forward

3 Way merging

Below image shows how the 3 way merge works in Git.
From master branch, we created new feature branch and
added 2 commits into it. Meanwhile master branch has
also got one new commit. In this case, merging is done by
creating new commit (after removing conflicts if any) and
pointing the HEAD to the new commit.

Before Merging

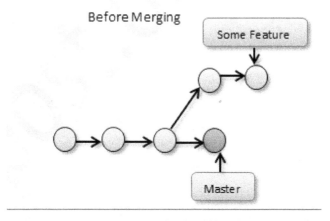

After a 3-way Merge

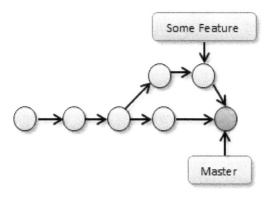

3 way merge in Git

In below image, we are trying to merge branch x into master branch. But since there are conflicts, fast forward merge is not possible. In this case, you can use git status command to view what files are in conflict, resolve those conflicts and finally commit the changes.

```
Sagar@Sagar-Windows10 MINGW64 ~/gitproject (master)
$ git merge x
Auto-merging f1.txt
CONFLICT (content): Merge conflict in f1.txt
Automatic merge failed; fix conflicts and then commit the result.

Sagar@Sagar-Windows10 MINGW64 ~/gitproject (master|MERGING)
$ git status
On branch master
Your branch is ahead of 'myorigin/master' by 3 commits.
  (use "git push" to publish your local commits)
You have unmerged paths.
  (fix conflicts and run "git commit")

Changes to be committed:

        new file:   abc
        new file:   x.txt

Unmerged paths:
  (use "git add <file>..." to mark resolution)

        both modified:   f1.txt
```

3 way merge when there is a conflict

17.4 Resolving conflicts

When merging the branches, we often come across the conflicts. When same files are changes in both branches, conflicts occur.

Viewing the conflicts

When merging the branch, we get error message saying
there is conflict as shown below. We can also view the files
that are in conflict using git status command. Below image
shows that in both branches (x and master), file f1.txt has
been changed.

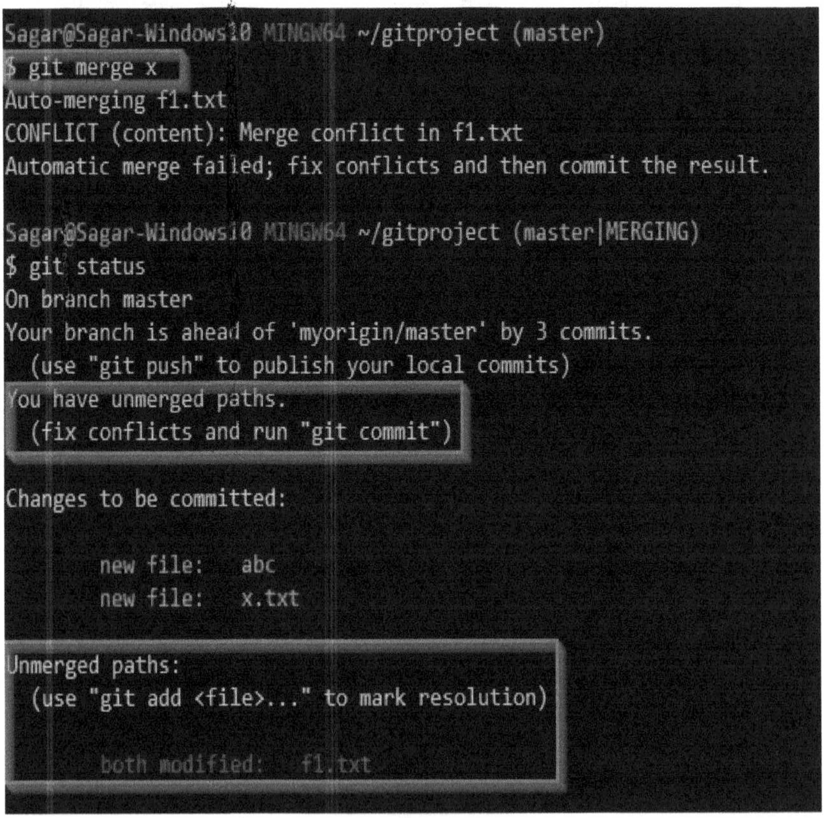

```
Sagar@Sagar-Windows10 MINGW64 ~/gitproject (master)
$ git merge x
Auto-merging f1.txt
CONFLICT (content): Merge conflict in f1.txt
Automatic merge failed; fix conflicts and then commit the result.

Sagar@Sagar-Windows10 MINGW64 ~/gitproject (master|MERGING)
$ git status
On branch master
Your branch is ahead of 'myorigin/master' by 3 commits.
  (use "git push" to publish your local commits)
You have unmerged paths.
  (fix conflicts and run "git commit")

Changes to be committed:

        new file:   abc
        new file:   x.txt

Unmerged paths:
  (use "git add <file>..." to mark resolution)

        both modified:   f1.txt
```

3 way merge when there is a conflict

To view the conflicts in specific file, use below command.
Changes made in local copy are shown between <<<<<<<

HEAD and =======. Changes made in other branch are shown between ======= and >>>>>>>

After resolving the conflict, you have to add the files into staging area and commit the changes. When all conflicts are resolved and committed, merging process is finished.

Viewing the conflicts in specific file in Git

17.5 Rebase

Rebase is one of the branch merging strategy in Git.

With 3 way merge strategy, git history becomes non-linear. But with rebase, Git history becomes linear. With rebase, commits of feature branch are played on the top of main branch thus creating a linear history.

Below command will play the commits (up to common parent of both branches) of currently checked out branch on the top of feature_branch.

git rebase feature_branch

Below image would be useful in understanding the Git Rebase command. Here we are playing the commits of local branch (S and T) on the top of remote branch (Q and R).

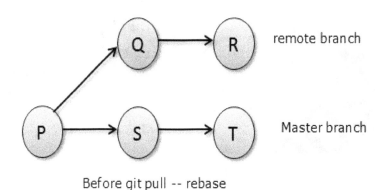

Before git pull -- rebase

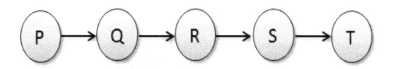

After git pull -- rebase

git rebase

17.6 Deleting branches

Deleting local branches

You can delete the branch in git using below command.

git branch -d branch_name

If the branch you are deleting has some un-merged changes, you will not be allowed to delete the branch.

To force delete the branch, you can use below command.

git branch -D branch_name

Deleting remote branches

git push origin --delete branch_name

17.7 Renaming the branch

You can rename the local branch using below syntax.

git branch -m new_branch_name

18. Collaborating with team

18.1 Push

To work with remote repository, you need to use push and pull commands as shown in below image.

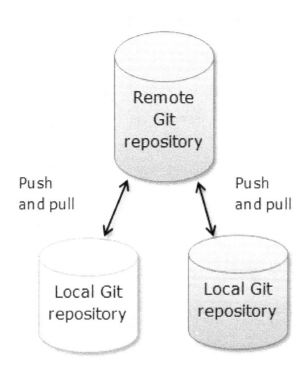

push and pull in git

We can push the local changes to remote repository using below command.

git push -u origin master

```
$ git push
Counting objects: 11, done.
Delta compression using up to 4 threads.
Compressing objects: 100% (7/7), done.
Writing objects: 100% (11/11), 1016 bytes | 0 bytes/s, done.
Total 11 (delta 2), reused 0 (delta 0)
To https://github.com/reply2sagar/gitproject.git
   5631fb6..bfce6b2  master -> master
```

git push

If you want to push the current branch to new remote branch, you can use below command. Notice that below command will create new branch locally as well as in remote repository.

git push -u origin b1

```
Sagar@Sagar-Windows10 MINGW64 ~/gitproject (master)
$ git push -u myorigin b1
Total 0 (delta 0), reused 0 (delta 0)
To https://github.com/reply2sagar/gitproject.git
 * [new branch]      b1 -> b1
Branch b1 set up to track remote branch b1 from myorigin.
```

pushing to different branch in git

18.2 Pull

To update the your local repository with remote changes, you will have to use pull command.

git pull

git pull command is equivalent to git fetch + git merge command. So when you are pulling the changes, you are not only getting the changes from remote repository to your local repository but you are merging it as well with your local copy.

```
Sagar@Sagar-Windows10 MINGW64 ~/gitproject (master)
$ git pull
remote: Counting objects: 3, done.
remote: Compressing objects: 100% (2/2), done.
remote: Total 3 (delta 0), reused 0 (delta 0), pack-reused 0
Unpacking objects: 100% (3/3), done.
From https://github.com/reply2sagar/gitproject
   bfce6b2..db1a0b4  master      -> myorigin/master
Updating bfce6b2..db1a0b4
Fast-forward
 abc | 1 +
 1 file changed, 1 insertion(+)
```

git pull

19. Stashing the changes in Git

We often need to switch branches while working on different features or bug fixes. Most of the times we are in the middle of changing something on Branch A and suddenly we need to switch to different branch to fix something that is very urgent.

In such situations, we are not in a position to commit the changes as we have not finished the development yet in current branch. If we switch to the different branch, uncommitted changes are also seen in other branch which we usually do not want. So what to do in these situations?

That's when Git stash comes into picture. We can stash the uncommitted changes which puts the branch in last commit status and working directory becomes clean. Then we can safely switch to other branch, complete the work in that branch then switch to back earlier branch and get the stashed changes back to the working directory.

Below image shows that we have modified the file f1.txt in master branch.

```
$ git status
On branch master
Your branch is ahead of 'origin/master' by 1 commit.
  (use "git push" to publish your local commits)
Changes not staged for commit:
  (use "git add <file>..." to update what will be committed)
  (use "git checkout -- <file>..." to discard changes in working directory)

      modified:   f1.txt

no changes added to commit (use "git add" and/or "git commit -a")
```

uncommitted changes in Git

Below image shows that we have switched to branch b1
and the changes from master branch are also visible there.
We do not want that...So let us use stash.

```
$ git branch
  b1
* master

Sagar@Sagar-Windows10 MINGW64 ~/gitproject (master)
$ git checkout b1
M       f1.txt
Switched to branch 'b1'

Sagar@Sagar-Windows10 MINGW64 ~/gitproject (b1)
$ git status
On branch b1
Changes not staged for commit:
  (use "git add <file>..." to update what will be committed)
  (use "git checkout -- <file>..." to discard changes in working directory)

      modified:   f1.txt

no changes added to commit (use "git add" and/or "git commit -a")
```

new branch also shows the same changes as
earlier branch

65

To save the changes in stash, you can use below command.

git stash save "stash1"

Stash command in Git

After putting the changes on stash, working directory gets clean and you can switch to other branch and after finishing work in other branch you can come back to main branch. Then we can apply the stash so that saved changes would appear in working directory.

Applying the stash

To apply the most recent stash, you can use below command.

git stash apply

To apply the specific stash, you can use below command.

git stash apply stash@{2}

Below image shows the above command in action.

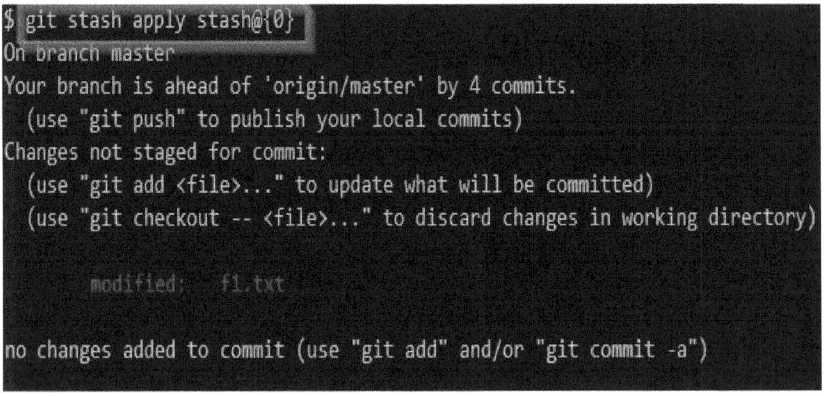

```
$ git stash apply stash@{0}
On branch master
Your branch is ahead of 'origin/master' by 4 commits.
  (use "git push" to publish your local commits)
Changes not staged for commit:
  (use "git add <file>..." to update what will be committed)
  (use "git checkout -- <file>..." to discard changes in working directory)

        modified:   f1.txt

no changes added to commit (use "git add" and/or "git commit -a")
```

Applying stash in Git

Clearing the stash items

When you apply the stash, that stash is not removed from stash list. You can use below command to remove item from stash.

git stash drop stash@{1}

Below command applies the most recent stash and then removes it from stash

git stash pop

Viewing all items in stash

You can view all items in stash using below command.

git stash list

Clearing all entries in stash

You can clear all entries from stash using below command.

git stash clear

20. Tags in Git

Tags can be used to record the milestones or important releases in Git history.

There are 2 types of tags in Git.

1. Lightweight.
2. Annotated - In this type of tags, we can specify the author creating tags and also provide tag description.

Creating Lightweight tags

Now let us see how to create a lightweight tag. Below command creates a simple tag.

git tag v1.1

To view all tags on current branch, you can use below command.

git tag

git tag command

Creating Annotated tags

Now let us see how to create a annotated tag. Below command creates a annotated tag.

git tag -a v1.3 -m "version 1.3"

We can also tag specific commit using below command

git tag -a v1.4 347dh82

```
Sagar@Sagar-Windows10 MINGW64 ~/gitproject (master)
$ git tag -a v1.3 -m "annotated tag"

Sagar@Sagar-Windows10 MINGW64 ~/gitproject (master)
$ git tag
v1.0
v1.1
v1.3

Sagar@Sagar-Windows10 MINGW64 ~/gitproject (master)
$ git show v1.1
commit d79e2a0c3766a43ca9b6de1103dc01649fc94854
Author: sagar <sagar@softpost.com>
Date:   Thu Jun 30 18:07:25 2016 +1000
```

annotated tags in Git

We can push the tags to remote repository using below command.

git push origin v1.0

To check out specific tag in new branch, you can use below command. In below command, we are checking out tag - v1.0 to branch b4.

git checkout -b b4 v1.0

21. Patches in Git

In this topic, we will see how to create a patch file in Git and apply it to another repository.

Below image shows how to create a patch file in Git. In below example, we have switched to new branch - b5 , added one commit and then created a patch file for master branch.

```
$ git checkout -b b5
Switched to a new branch 'b5'

Sagar@Sagar-Windows10 MINGW64 ~/gitproject (b5)
$ echo "sdsdd" >> xyz

Sagar@Sagar-Windows10 MINGW64 ~/gitproject (b5)
$ git status
On branch b5
Untracked files:
  (use "git add <file>..." to include in what will be committed)

        xyz

nothing added to commit but untracked files present (use "git add" to tr

Sagar@Sagar-Windows10 MINGW64 ~/gitproject (b5)
$ git add .
warning: LF will be replaced by CRLF in xyz.
The file will have its original line endings in your working directory.

Sagar@Sagar-Windows10 MINGW64 ~/gitproject (b5)
$ git commit -m "added xyz"
[b5 367abfa] added xyz
warning: LF will be replaced by CRLF in xyz.
The file will have its original line endings in your working directory.
 1 file changed, 1 insertion(+)
 create mode 100644 xyz

Sagar@Sagar-Windows10 MINGW64 ~/gitproject (b5)
$ git format-patch master --stdout >> mypatch.patch

Sagar@Sagar-Windows10 MINGW64 ~/gitproject (b5)
$ ls
abc   f1.txt   g1   mypatch.patch   x.txt   xyz
```

Creating patch in Git

Applying a patch on master branch

Now let us see how to apply a patch to master branch.
First switch to master branch and execute commands as
displayed in below image.

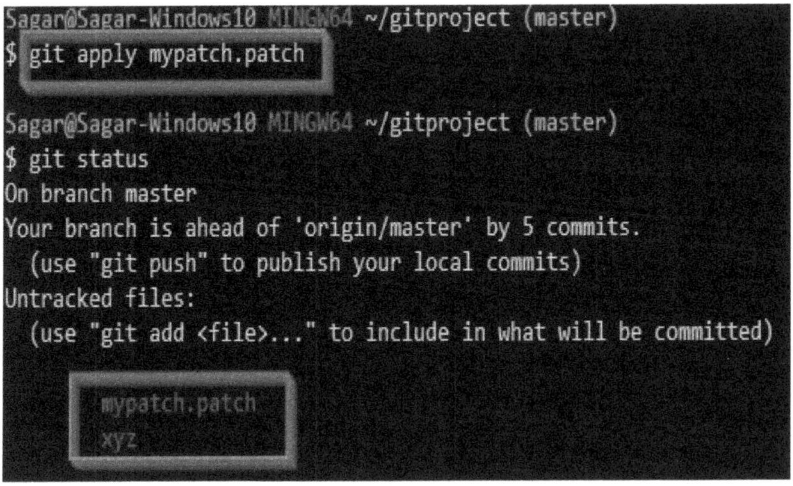

How to apply patch in Git

22. Working with GitHub project

22.1 Creating new repository on GitHub

Below images show how to create a new Git repository on GitHub.

Once you login to GitHub account, click on New Repository button.

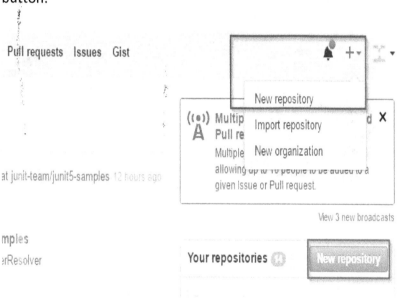

new repository on GitHub

On next page, you have to provide below details.

1. Repository name
2. Mention if it is public or private repository

Create a new repository

A repository contains all the files for your project, including the revision history.

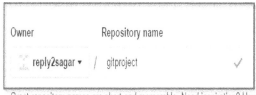

Great repository names are short and memorable. Need inspiration? How about ubiquitous-doodle.

Description (optional)

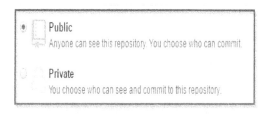

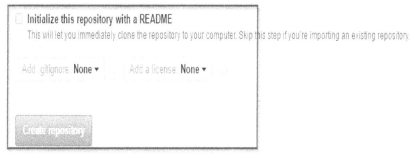

Creating new Git repository on GitHub

22.2 Pushing local repository to remote repository like GitHub

We have already seen how to initialize a local repository using Git. Now suppose you want to push this repository to remote repository on GitHub.

Below image shows how to add remote repository and push local repository to remote one.

In 2 steps, you can push the changes.

1. First register remote repository using **git remote add origin repository_url**

2. Then push the local repository changes to remote using **git push -u origin master** command. The meaning of this command is that push the local repository's current branch to the master branch of remote repository. -u switch sets the upstream branch permanently. So next time, you can just use **git push** command

```
Sagar@Sagar-Windows10 MINGW64 ~/gitproject (master)
$ git remote add origin https://github.com/reply2sagar/gitproject.git

Sagar@Sagar-Windows10 MINGW64 ~/gitproject (master)
$ git push -u origin master
Counting objects: 9, done.
Delta compression using up to 4 threads.
Compressing objects: 100% (5/5), done.
Writing objects: 100% (9/9), 727 bytes | 0 bytes/s, done.
Total 9 (delta 0), reused 0 (delta 0)
To https://github.com/reply2sagar/gitproject.git
 * [new branch]      master -> master
Branch master set up to track remote branch master from origin.
```

Pushing existing repository to GitHub repository

Note that by default remote repository is called as origin.

But you can rename it using below command.

git remote rename origin myorigin

23. Git integration

23.1 IntelliJ IDEA

IntelliJ IDEA provides very good support to Git.

We can perform all operations like adding files to staging area, committing changes, viewing Git log history, pushing and pulling the changes from remote repository etc.

Below image shows how to access Git window in IntelliJ IDEA.

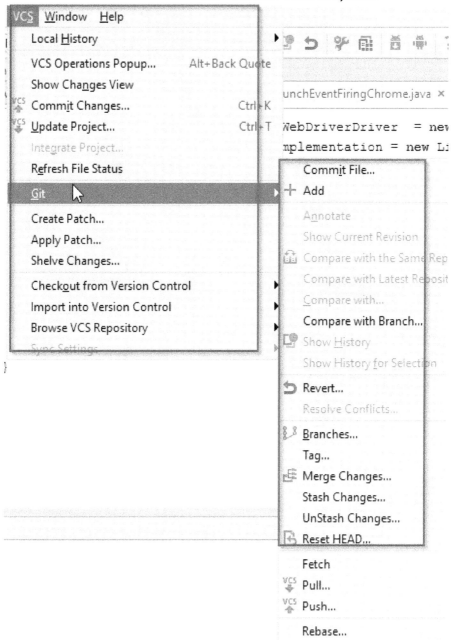

Git menu in IntelliJ IDEA

Below image shows how to commit changes. We can invoke below window using CTRL + K short cut key.

Git commit window in IntelliJ IDEA

Below image shows how to push the changes to remote repository. We can invoke this window using CTRL+SHIFT+K shortcut key.

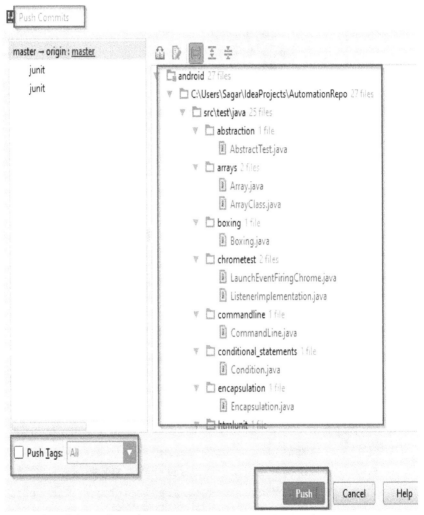

Pushing the changes to remote repository

Below image shows how to update project in Git. We can invoke this window using CTRL + T shortcut key.

83

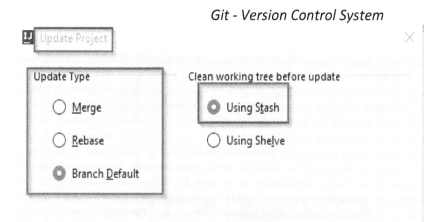

Pulling changes from remote git repository in IntelliJ IDEA

Below image shows how to view log of git history and local changes from version control window.

Version control window showing git log, local changes in IntelliJ IDEA

Below image shows how to manage branches in Git in IntelliJ IDEA.

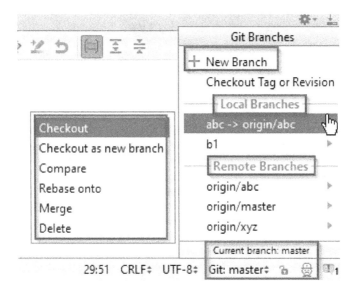

Managing branches in Git in IntelliJ IDEA

www.ingramcontent.com/pod-product-compliance
Lightning Source LLC
Chambersburg PA
CBHW061019050326
40689CB00012B/2679